MATH SMARTS!

Fraction and Decimal
SMARTS!

Lucille Caron
Philip M. St. Jacques

E Enslow Publishers, Inc.
40 Industrial Road
Box 398
Berkeley Heights, NJ 07922
USA
http://www.enslow.com

Original edition published as *Fractions and Decimals* in 2000.

Library of Congress Cataloging-in-Publication Data

Caron, Lucille.
  Fraction and decimal smarts! / Lucille Caron and Philip M. St. Jacques.
      p. cm. — (Math smarts!)
  Includes index.
  ISBN 978-0-7660-3936-0
  1. Fractions—Juvenile literature. 2. Decimal fractions—Juvenile literature. I. St.
Jacques, Philip M. II. Title.
  QA117.C369 2012
  513.2′6—dc22

                                                          2011008382

Paperback ISBN: 978-1-59845-321-8

Printed in China

052011 Leo Paper Group, Heshan City, Guangdong, China.

10 9 8 7 6 5 4 3 2 1

To Our Readers:
We have done our best to make sure all Internet addresses in this book were
active and appropriate when we went to press. However, the author and the
publisher have no control over and assume no liability for the material available
on those Internet sites or on other Web sites they may link to. Any comments or
suggestions can be sent by e-mail to comments@enslow.com or to the address
on the back cover.

Cover Illustration: Shutterstock.com

Contents

Introduction

If you were to look up the meaning of the word *mathematics*, you would find that it is the study of numbers, quantities, and shapes, and how they relate to each other.

Mathematics is important to all world cultures, including our world of work. Many people—teachers, parents, other family members, and friends—have explained to others why math should be studied. The following are just some of the ways in which studying math will help you:

▶ You will know how much money you are spending at the store.

▶ You will know if the cashier has given you the right change.

▶ You will know how to use measurements to build things.

▶ Your science classes will be easier and more interesting.

▶ You will understand music on a whole new level.

▶ You will be empowered to qualify for and land a rewarding job.

Fractions and decimals are an important part of math. Prices, in dollars and cents, are decimals. So are baseball and softball players' batting averages. Knowing fractions makes it possible to cook and bake enough food for two people or twenty.

This book has been written so that you can learn about fractions and decimals at your own speed. You can use this book on your own, or work together with a friend, tutor, or parent.

Good luck and have fun!

5

A fraction may represent a whole, part of a whole, or more than a whole.

$\frac{8}{8}$ $\frac{6}{8}$ $\frac{10}{8}$

whole   **part of a whole**   **more than a whole**

The symbol used to represent a fraction is called a fraction line or a fraction bar. It is usually represented by a horizontal line.

$$\frac{1}{2} \longleftarrow \textbf{fraction bar}$$

The top number of the fraction is called the numerator. The bottom number of the fraction is called the denominator.

$$\textbf{denominator} \longrightarrow \frac{4}{7} \longleftarrow \textbf{numerator}$$

The numerator is the number of parts you are looking at.
The denominator is the total number of parts in a whole.

The fraction $\frac{4}{7}$ is read as "four sevenths," or "four divided by seven." The bottom number, 7, tells you that the fraction has been divided into seven equal parts. The top number, 4, tells you how many parts you are looking at out of the total number of parts.

Pictorial Fractions

Pictorial fractions are used to illustrate fractions. You can represent the fraction $\frac{4}{7}$ by dividing a rectangle into seven equal parts and shading 4 of the parts.

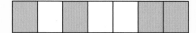

numerator — The number written *above* the fraction line.
denominator — The number written *below* the fraction line.
(Remember, the **d**enominator is **d**own.)

Proper Fractions

A proper fraction is a fraction whose numerator (top number) is less than its denominator (bottom number).

$$\frac{3}{4} \qquad \frac{1}{2} \qquad \frac{7}{8}$$

What fraction of a year is five months?

January	February	March	
April	**May**	June	$\frac{5}{12}$
July	August	September	
October	November	December	

The bottom number of the fraction stands for the total number of months in a year. The top number stands for five months of the year. $\frac{5}{12}$ is a proper fraction.

Improper Fractions

An improper fraction is a fraction whose numerator is larger than or equal to its denominator.

$$\frac{9}{9} \qquad \frac{3}{2} \qquad \frac{6}{3}$$

$\frac{9}{9}$ is an improper fraction because the numerator is equal to the denominator. $\frac{3}{2}$ and $\frac{6}{3}$ are also improper fractions because the numerators are greater than the denominators.

Mixed Numbers

A mixed number contains two parts: a whole number other than zero and a fraction.

$$6\frac{3}{7} \qquad 2\frac{1}{2} \qquad 8\frac{5}{9}$$

Mixed numbers, such as $6\frac{3}{7}$, can be written as improper fractions. Multiply the whole number by the denominator ($6 \times 7 = 42$). Then add the numerator to the product ($42 + 3 = 45$) and place the sum over the denominator ($\frac{45}{7}$). So, $6\frac{3}{7} = \frac{45}{7}$.

Proper fractions represent part of a whole.
Whole numbers are the numbers: 0, 1, 2, 3, ...
A product is the answer in a multiplication problem.

Out of 18 sections in a baseball stadium, 9 sections are reserved. One of your friends says that $\frac{9}{18}$ of the sections are reserved. Your other friend says that $\frac{1}{2}$ are reserved. Who is correct? To find out, divide a rectangle into 18 equal squares. Shade in nine of the squares.

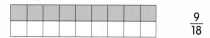 $\frac{9}{18}$

Nine out of eighteen squares are shaded.

Now take the same sized rectangle and divide it in half to represent your other friend's claim that $\frac{1}{2}$ of the seats are reserved. Shade in one section.

 $\frac{1}{2}$

In both rectangles, $\frac{1}{2}$ of the figure is shaded. Nine eighteenths ($\frac{9}{18}$) and one half ($\frac{1}{2}$) name the same amount. Fractions that name the same amount are called equivalent fractions.

Finding Equivalent Fractions

Find an equivalent fraction for $\frac{1}{2}$.

Step 1: Choose any number you wish. Suppose you chose 9.

Step 2: Multiply the numerator and denominator by 9.

$$\frac{1}{2} \times \frac{9}{9} = \frac{1 \times 9}{2 \times 9} = \frac{9}{18}$$

Multiplying the numerator and the denominator by the same number, such as 9, is the same as multiplying the original fraction by 1 (since $\frac{9}{9} = 1$). It does not change the value.

Step 3: Write the equivalent fraction. $\frac{1}{2} = \frac{9}{18}$

$\frac{1}{2}$ is equivalent to $\frac{9}{18}$. An equal sign (=) is used to represent equivalent fractions.

Reducing Fractions to Lowest Terms

A fraction is in lowest terms if both the numerator and denominator cannot be divided by any number except one.

Reduce $\frac{9}{18}$ to lowest terms.

Step 1: List the factors of 9:　　　　1, 3, **9**

List the factors of 18:　　　　1, 2, 3, 6, **9**, 18

1, 3, and 9 are all factors of both numbers, but 9 is the largest. It is called the greatest common factor (GCF).

Step 2: Divide the numerator and denominator by the GCF.

$$\frac{9 \div \mathbf{9}}{18 \div \mathbf{9}} = \frac{1}{2}$$

Step 3: Write the fraction in lowest terms.

$$\frac{9}{18} = \frac{1}{2}$$

Renaming a fraction in higher terms requires *multiplying* both the numerator and denominator by the same number. Renaming a fraction in lowest terms requires *dividing* both the numerator and denominator by the greatest common factor.

That's cool.

factors — Those numbers that divide exactly into a number.
greatest common factor (GCF) — The largest number that divides evenly into a set of numbers.

3 Comparing and Ordering Fractions

You can compare fractions if the denominators are the same. Fractions with the same denominators are called *like fractions*. The following symbols are used to compare numbers:

That's good to know.

symbol	meaning
<	is less than
>	is greater than
=	is equal to

Compare $\frac{1}{3}$ and $\frac{2}{3}$

Both fractions have the same denominator, 3. That means that $\frac{1}{3}$ and $\frac{2}{3}$ are like fractions. Now compare the numerators.

Since 1 is less than 2, $\frac{1}{3} < \frac{2}{3}$

The symbol points to the number that is smaller.

Comparing Unlike Fractions

Compare $\frac{2}{5}$ and $\frac{1}{3}$

Step 1: To change unlike fractions into like fractions, list the multiples of the denominators, 3 and 5.

multiples of 3:   3, 6, 9, 12, **15**, . . .

multiples of 5:   5, 10, **15**, 20, . . .

The least common multiple (LCM) is 15. 15 will be the new denominator for both fractions.

To find the **multiples** of 3, count by 3s: 3, 6, 9, 12, 15, . . .
To find the **multiples** of 5, count by 5s: 5, 10, 15, 20, . . .

Step 2: Find the new numerator for both fractions.

$$\frac{2}{5} = \frac{?}{15} \qquad \frac{1}{3} = \frac{?}{15}$$

How many 5s are there in 15? There are 3. Multiply 2×3 to get the new numerator. $\qquad \frac{2 \times 3}{5 \times 3} = \frac{6}{15}, \qquad$ so $\frac{2}{5} = \frac{6}{15}$

How many 3s are there in 15? There are 5. Multiply 1×5.

$$\frac{1 \times 5}{3 \times 5} = \frac{5}{15}, \qquad \text{so } \frac{1}{3} = \frac{5}{15}$$

Step 3: Compare the numerators. $\qquad \frac{6}{15} > \frac{5}{15}$, so $\frac{2}{3} > \frac{1}{3}$

Ordering Fractions

Order $\frac{1}{2}, \frac{1}{3}, \frac{1}{4},$ and $\frac{5}{6}$

Step 1: Find the LCM for all the denominators.

multiples of 2: 2, 4, 6, 8, 10, **12**, 14, . . .

multiples of 3: 3, 6, 9, **12**, 15, . . .

multiples of 4: 4, 8, **12**, 16, . . .

multiples of 6: 6, **12**, 18, 24, . . . The LCM is 12.

Step 2: Write equivalent fractions with the new denominator, 12.

$$\frac{1}{2} = \frac{1 \times 6}{2 \times 6} = \frac{6}{12} \qquad \frac{1}{3} = \frac{1 \times 4}{3 \times 4} = \frac{4}{12}$$

$$\frac{1}{4} = \frac{1 \times 3}{4 \times 3} = \frac{3}{12} \qquad \frac{5}{6} = \frac{5 \times 2}{6 \times 2} = \frac{10}{12}$$

Step 3: Compare and order the numerators. $3 < 4 < 6 < 10$

Step 4: Write the original fractions in order from least to greatest. $\qquad \frac{1}{4}, \frac{1}{3}, \frac{1}{2}, \frac{5}{6}$

When you look at multiples of some numbers, the **common multiples** are in the sets of multiples for each number. The **least common multiple (LCM)** is the smallest of these.

Renaming Fractions as Decimals

You can use 100 pennies to change a fraction to a decimal.

Change the fraction $\frac{1}{10}$ to a decimal.

The denominator tells you how many equal groups of pennies you need to make.

Separate 100 pennies into 10 equal groups and count the pennies in one group. There should be 10 pennies, or 10 cents, in one group. $\frac{1}{10} = \frac{10}{100} = 0.10$

Change the fraction $\frac{3}{4}$ to a decimal.

Separate 100 pennies into four equal groups. The numerator (3) tells you how many groups to count out of the total number of groups. Count how many pennies there are in three groups.

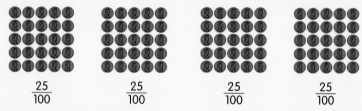

$\frac{25}{100}$ $\frac{25}{100}$ $\frac{25}{100}$ $\frac{25}{100}$

How many pennies are in each group? (25) How many pennies are in three groups? (75)

You can write seventy-five cents as $0.75. Three fourths is the same as 0.75. $\frac{3}{4} = \frac{75}{100} = 0.75$

A **decimal fraction** has a denominator of 10, 100, 1000, or other multiple of 10. Examples: $\frac{2}{10}$ or $\frac{18}{100}$. They can be easily turned into decimal numbers: $\frac{2}{10} = 0.2$ or $\frac{18}{100} = 0.18$

Here is another way to rename a fraction as a decimal:

Change the fraction $\frac{2}{3}$ to a decimal.

Step 1: Divide the denominator into the numerator.

$$3\overline{)2} \longleftarrow \textbf{dividend}$$

Step 2: Place a decimal point to the right of the number in the dividend and add a zero. Place the decimal point in the quotient directly above the decimal point in the dividend.

$$. \longleftarrow \textbf{quotient}$$
$$3\overline{)2.0} \longleftarrow \textbf{dividend}$$

Step 3: Divide. How many 3s are there in two? (0)
How many 3s are there in 20? (6)
Multiply ($6 \times 3 = 18$).
Subtract ($20 - 18 = 2$).

$$\begin{array}{r} 0.6 \\ 3\overline{)2.0} \\ -18 \\ \hline 2 \end{array} \leftarrow \textbf{remainder}$$

Step 4: Add another zero in the dividend. Bring down the zero. Divide 3 into the remainder, 20.

$$\begin{array}{r} 0.66 \\ 3\overline{)2.00} \\ -18 \\ \hline 20 \\ -18 \\ \hline 2 \end{array} \longleftarrow \textbf{remainder}$$

This isn't so hard.

If you continue dividing, the remainder will always be 2 and the digit 6 will repeat in the quotient. 0.66 . . . is a repeating decimal. One way to write a repeating decimal is to put a bar over the digit or digits that repeat. $\frac{2}{3} = 0.\overline{6}$

You rename fractions as decimals every day. When you spend a **quarter**, or $\frac{1}{4}$ dollar, you spend $0.25, or twenty-five cents.

Adding Like Fractions

Suppose you cut a pizza pie into thirds and gave your two best friends one piece of the pie each. How much of the whole pizza do they have?

Estimating Like Fractions

Before you find the actual sum, estimate the sum so you will have an idea of what the answer should be.

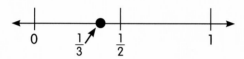

You can use a number line to estimate the sum of $\frac{1}{3} + \frac{1}{3}$.

$$\frac{1}{2} + \frac{1}{2} = 1 \qquad \frac{1}{3} < \frac{1}{2}. \qquad \text{Therefore, } \frac{1}{3} + \frac{1}{3} < 1.$$

You know the answer will be less than 1.

Adding Two Like Fractions

Now add $\frac{1}{3} + \frac{1}{3}$

Add the numerators. Place the sum over the denominator.

$$\frac{1 + 1}{3} = \frac{2}{3}$$

Your two best friends have two thirds of the pie.

Adding Whole Numbers and Fractions

A mixed number is a whole number and a proper fraction. To add a whole number and a fraction, put them together as a mixed number.

$$1 + \frac{1}{2} = 1\frac{1}{2} \qquad 5 + \frac{7}{8} = 5\frac{7}{8}$$

Remember: Fractions that have the same denominators are called **like fractions**.

Adding Two Mixed Numbers

Add $1\frac{1}{8} + 2\frac{5}{8}$

Step 1: Add the whole numbers. Add the numerators and place the sum over the denominator.

I can do this.

$$\begin{array}{r} 1\frac{1}{8} \\ + 2\frac{5}{8} \\ \hline 3\frac{6}{8} \end{array}$$

Step 2: Reduce the fraction $3\frac{6}{8}$ to lowest terms. Divide the numerator and denominator by the greatest common factor. $3\frac{6 \div 2}{8 \div 2} = 3\frac{3}{4}$

Adding Mixed Numbers and Fractions

Add $3\frac{4}{9} + \frac{5}{9} + 4\frac{1}{9}$

Step 1: Add the whole numbers. Add the numerators and place the sum over the denominator.

Step 2: Reduce the fraction $7\frac{10}{9}$ to lowest terms. Divide 10 by 9.

Step 3: Add.

$$7 + 1\frac{1}{9} = 8\frac{1}{9}$$

$$\begin{array}{r} 3\frac{4}{9} \\ \frac{5}{9} \\ + 4\frac{1}{9} \\ \hline 7\frac{10}{9} \end{array}$$

$$\begin{array}{r} 1 \\ 9\overline{)10} = 1\frac{1}{9} \\ -9 \\ \hline 1 \end{array}$$

The greatest common factor (GCF) is the largest number that will evenly divide both the numerator and denominator. See page 9 for an example.

Does your community recycle aluminum cans, plastics, newspaper, or glass? Do any of your friends collect recyclables and bring them to a recycling center in exchange for money?

Suppose your community recycling center paid you for every pound of aluminum, plastic, paper, and glass you recycled. If you recycled $\frac{2}{3}$ pound of newspapers, $2\frac{3}{4}$ pounds of aluminum cans, and $3\frac{5}{6}$ pounds of glass, for how many pounds of recyclables would the recycling center pay you?

Adding Mixed Numbers and Fractions with Unlike Denominators

Add $\frac{2}{3} + 2\frac{3}{4} + 3\frac{5}{6}$

Remember, to add mixed numbers and fractions, you need a common denominator.

Step 1: Find the least common multiple (LCM) of 3, 4, and 6.

multiples of 3:	3, 6, 9, **12**, 15, . . .
multiples of 4:	4, 8, **12**, 16, . . .
multiples of 6:	6, **12**, 18, 24, . . .

The LCM is 12.

unlike fractions — Fractions with different denominators.
mixed number — A number that is a whole number with a fraction.

Step 2: The LCM (12) becomes the least common denominator (LCD). Write equivalent fractions.

$$\frac{2}{3} = \frac{2 \times 4}{3 \times 4} = \frac{8}{12}$$

$$\frac{3}{4} = \frac{3 \times 3}{4 \times 3} = \frac{9}{12}$$

$$\frac{5}{6} = \frac{5 \times 2}{6 \times 2} = \frac{10}{12}$$

Step 3: Add the whole numbers and the fractions.

$$\frac{2}{3} = \frac{8}{12}$$
$$2\frac{3}{4} = 2\frac{9}{12}$$
$$+ 3\frac{5}{6} = + 3\frac{10}{12}$$
$$\overline{\hspace{2cm} 5\frac{27}{12}}$$

Step 4: Reduce the sum to lowest terms.

$$\begin{array}{r} 2 \\ 12\overline{)27} \\ -24 \\ \hline 3 \end{array}$$

$$\frac{27}{12} = 2\frac{3}{12} = 2\frac{3 \div 3}{12 \div 3} = 2\frac{1}{4}$$

$$5\frac{27}{12} = 5 + 2\frac{1}{4} = 7\frac{1}{4}$$

You recycled $7\frac{1}{4}$ pounds of recyclables.

If you want to know how much money you could make by recycling, rename your fraction (pounds) as a decimal (see page 13), then multiply this number by the price per pound.

---

equivalent fractions — Fractions that name the same number. For example, $\frac{8}{12}$ and $\frac{6}{9}$ both equal $\frac{2}{3}$. So, $\frac{8}{12}$ and $\frac{6}{9}$ are equivalent fractions.

Of a dozen eggs, suppose you had 11 eggs left. If you use 3 of those to make scrambled eggs for breakfast, what fractional part of the original dozen eggs would you have left?

Subtract $\frac{11}{12} - \frac{3}{12}$

Step 1: Subtract the numerators and place the difference over the denominator.

$$\frac{11 - 3}{12} = \frac{8}{12}$$

Step 2: Find the greatest common factor (GCF) of 8 and 12.

factors of 8:   1, 2, **4**, 8

factors of 12:   1, 2, 3, **4**, 6, 12   GCF = 4

Step 3: Reduce the fraction by this greatest common factor.

$$\frac{8}{12} = \frac{8 \div 4}{12 \div 4} = \frac{2}{3}$$

You would have $\frac{2}{3}$ of a dozen eggs left.

Subtracting a Fraction from a Whole Number

To subtract a fraction from a whole number, rename the whole number as a fraction or mixed number. For example, suppose you ate $\frac{3}{12}$ of one pie. One pie also equals $\frac{12}{12}$ pie.

$\frac{12}{12} - \frac{3}{12} = \frac{9}{12}$ and $\frac{9 \div 3}{12 \div 3} = \frac{3}{4}$

$\frac{3}{4}$ of the pie is left.

Dividing the numerator and the denominator by the same number, such as 3, is the same as dividing the original fraction by 1 (since $\frac{3}{3} = 1$). It does not change the value.

Subtract $4 - \frac{5}{6}$

Step 1: Rename 4 as a mixed number. To do this, subtract 1 from the whole number 4.

$$4 - 1 = 3$$

Write the 1 as a fraction with the same denominator as $\frac{5}{6}$.

$$1 = \frac{6}{6} \qquad 4 = 3 + \frac{6}{6} = 3\frac{6}{6}$$

Step 2: Subtract numerators. Bring down the whole number.

$$
\begin{array}{cc}
4 = & 3\frac{6}{6} \\
-\frac{5}{6} = & -\frac{5}{6} \\
\hline
& 3\frac{1}{6}
\end{array}
$$

Cool move!

Subtracting Two Mixed Numbers

Subtract $6\frac{1}{4} - 2\frac{3}{4}$

Since the numerator 3 is greater than the numerator 1, you will have to regroup the whole number 6.

Step 1: Rename $6\frac{1}{4}$.

$$6\frac{1}{4} = 5\frac{4}{4} + \frac{1}{4} = 5\frac{5}{4}$$

Step 2: Subtract numerators and bring down the denominator. Subtract whole numbers. Reduce to lowest terms.

$$
\begin{array}{c}
5\frac{5}{4} \\
-2\frac{3}{4} \\
\hline
3\frac{2}{4} = 3\frac{1}{2}
\end{array}
$$

Regrouping the whole number in a mixed fraction is similar to regrouping tens in simple whole-number subtraction problems, such as $21 - 9$.

Have you ever been in a hot-air balloon? Did you know that the higher you go, the farther you can see? If you are 1,000 feet above the ground, you can see a distance of $38\frac{3}{4}$ miles. At 50 feet above the ground, you can see a distance of $8\frac{1}{2}$ miles. How many more miles can you see at 1,000 feet than at 50 feet?

Subtraction of Two Mixed Numbers

Subtract $38\frac{3}{4} - 8\frac{1}{2}$

Step 1: Find the least common multiple (LCM) to make like fractions.

multiples of 2:	**2**, **4**, 6, 8, . . .
multiples of 4:	**4**, 8, 12, . . .

$$LCM = 4$$

Step 2: Find equivalent fractions by placing the LCM in the denominator. How many 2s are there in 4?

$$\frac{1}{2} = \frac{?}{4} \qquad \frac{1}{2} = \frac{2}{4}$$

Step 3: Subtract numerators and bring down the denominator. Subtract whole numbers.

$$\begin{array}{r} 38\frac{3}{4} = \quad 38\frac{3}{4} \\ -\ 8\frac{1}{2} = -\ 8\frac{2}{4} \\ \hline 30\frac{1}{4} \end{array}$$

You can see $30\frac{1}{4}$ more miles at 1,000 feet than at 50 feet.

Placing the LCM in the denominator of two fractions makes it the least common denominator (LCD).

Subtracting a Fraction from a Mixed Number

Subtract $3\frac{1}{5} - \frac{2}{3}$

Step 1: Find the least common denominator (LCD).

multiples of 3:   3, 6, 9, 12, **15**. . .

multiples of 5:   5, 10, **15**, 20 . . .

$$LCD = 15$$

Step 2: Find equivalent fractions using the LCD.

$$\frac{1}{5} = \frac{1 \times 3}{5 \times 3} = \frac{3}{15} \qquad\qquad \frac{2}{3} = \frac{2 \times 5}{3 \times 5} = \frac{10}{15}$$

Step 3: Borrow one from the whole number and add this to the original fraction. Express one as $\frac{15}{15}$.

$$3\frac{3}{15} = 2\frac{15}{15} + \frac{3}{15}$$

Step 4: Add $2\frac{15}{15} + \frac{3}{15}$.

$$2\frac{15}{15} + \frac{3}{15} = 2\frac{18}{15}$$

Step 5: Subtract the numerators. Bring down the whole number.

$$\begin{array}{r} 2\frac{18}{15} \\ - \frac{10}{15} \\ \hline 2\frac{8}{15} \end{array}$$

This answer is in lowest terms.

The answer is already in its lowest terms because there is no factor that can be divided evenly into both the numerator and the denominator.

When you subtract a fraction from a whole or mixed number, think of the fraction as having a "0" in the ones column.

Chefs take math courses when they learn how to cook. They use multiplication of fractions and mixed numbers when they have to double, triple, or take one half or one third of a recipe.

Sometimes a chef only has to make half a pie. How would the chef cut the following recipe in half?

Peanut Butter Jelly Marshmallow Pie (serves 6 people)

$2\frac{1}{4}$ cups peanut butter $\frac{1}{3}$ cup marshmallows

$1\frac{1}{2}$ cups jelly   1 tsp. salt

$1\frac{1}{3}$ cups sugar $\frac{1}{8}$ tsp. baking powder

$\frac{2}{3}$ cup shortening   2 cups flour

Multiplying Fractions

The chef decided to first cut the amount of marshmallows in half. To take $\frac{1}{2}$ of $\frac{1}{3}$ cup of marshmallows means the same as $\frac{1}{2} \times \frac{1}{3}$. The *of* means "multiply." To help you see $\frac{1}{2} \times \frac{1}{3}$, use a piece of paper.

   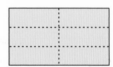

Fold the paper in half.   Then fold it into thirds.

Open the paper and shade in half of one of the three sections.

What fraction of the paper did you shade?

So, $\frac{1}{2} \times \frac{1}{3} = \frac{1}{6}$.

You can cancel or reduce fractions before or after you multiply. Canceling before multiplying saves you a step.

Multiplying a Fraction and a Mixed Number

How much sugar does the chef need to make half a pie?

Multiply $\frac{1}{2} \times 1\frac{1}{3}$

Step 1: Change the mixed number to an improper fraction. Multiply the whole number by the denominator. Add this product to the numerator and place the sum over the denominator.

$$1\frac{1}{3} = \frac{(1 \times 3) + 1}{3}$$
$$= \frac{3 + 1}{3}$$
$$= \frac{4}{3}$$

Step 2: To cancel or reduce fractions, find the greatest common factor (GCF) that will evenly divide the numerator and denominator.

$$\text{GCF} = 2$$
$$\frac{1}{{}_1\cancel{2}} \times \frac{\cancel{4}^{\,2}}{3}$$

Step 3: Multiply numerators. Multiply denominators.

$$\frac{1 \times 2}{1 \times 3} = \frac{2}{3}$$

For half a pie, the chef needs $\frac{2}{3}$ cup of sugar.

Multiplying a Whole Number and a Mixed Number

How much peanut butter would the chef need if he wanted to double the recipe?

Multiply $2 \times 2\frac{1}{4}$

Step 1: Write the whole number as a fraction by placing it over one. Change $2\frac{1}{4}$ to an improper fraction.

$$\frac{2}{1} \times \frac{9}{4}$$

Step 2: Reduce before multiplying.

$$\frac{{}^1\cancel{2}}{1} \times \frac{9}{\cancel{4}_2} = \frac{9}{2} = 4\frac{1}{2}$$

The chef would need $4\frac{1}{2}$ cups of peanut butter.

---

improper fraction — A fraction whose numerator is larger than its denominator, such as $\frac{16}{13}$ or $\frac{9}{5}$.

Reciprocals are used to divide fractions. The reciprocal of a fraction is found by switching the numerator and the denominator.

Find the reciprocal of $\frac{5}{8}$.

Switch the numerator and the denominator.

$\frac{5}{8} \diagdown \diagup \frac{8}{5}$ The reciprocal of $\frac{5}{8}$ is $\frac{8}{5}$.

The product of a fraction and its reciprocal is one.

$$\frac{5}{8} \times \frac{8}{5} = \frac{40}{40} = 1$$

Dividing a Fraction by a Fraction

How many quarters are there in one half?

Divide $\frac{1}{2}$ by $\frac{1}{4}$ $\frac{1}{2} \div \frac{1}{4}$

Step 1: Find the reciprocal of the second fraction ($\frac{1}{4}$).

The reciprocal of $\frac{1}{4}$ is $\frac{4}{1}$.

Step 2: Multiply the first fraction ($\frac{1}{2}$) by the reciprocal.

$$\frac{1}{2} \times \frac{4}{1} = \frac{1 \times 4}{2 \times 1} = \frac{4}{2}$$

Step 3: Reduce the fraction to lowest terms. How many 2s are there in 4? (2) $\frac{4}{2} = 2$

There are 2 quarters in one half.

The reciprocal of a whole number x is the number $\frac{1}{x}$.
For example, the reciprocal of 6 is $\frac{1}{6}$.
The reciprocal of $\frac{10}{4}$ is $\frac{4}{10}$.

Dividing a Whole Number by a Mixed Number

Your best friend wants to make shelves out of an 18-foot board. Suppose your friend wanted each shelf to be one foot long. How many shelves could she make? Divide 18 feet by 1 foot ($18 \div 1 = 18$). She could make 18 one-foot shelves from an 18-foot board. Now, suppose she wants each shelf to be $1\frac{1}{2}$ feet long.

Divide 18 by $1\frac{1}{2}$ $18 \div 1\frac{1}{2}$

Step 1: Write the mixed number as an improper fraction.

$$1\frac{1}{2} = \frac{(1 \times 2) + 1}{2} = \frac{2 + 1}{2} = \frac{3}{2}$$

$$18 \div 1\frac{1}{2} \text{ becomes } 18 \div \frac{3}{2}$$

Step 2: Find the reciprocal of the improper fraction.

The reciprocal of $\frac{3}{2}$ is $\frac{2}{3}$.

Step 3: Write the whole number as a fraction.

$$18 = \frac{18}{1}$$

Step 4: Write the multiplication problem.

$$\frac{18}{1} \times \frac{2}{3}$$

Step 5: Reduce fractions by the greatest common factor before multiplying.

$$\frac{18}{1} \times \frac{2}{3} = \frac{6\cancel{18}}{1} \times \frac{2}{\cancel{3}_1}$$

Step 6: Multiply numerators. Multiply denominators.

$$\frac{6 \times 2}{1 \times 1} = \frac{12}{1}$$

Step 7: Reduce to lowest terms.

$$\frac{12}{1} = 12$$

She can make 12 shelves that are $1\frac{1}{2}$ feet long.

See page 23 to review writing a mixed number as an improper fraction.

Estimation is used for everything from estimating the cost of a lunch to conducting surveys. Survey five of your friends and ask them how tall they are. Estimate their average height in feet. Suppose your friends' heights are $5\frac{3}{4}$ feet, $4\frac{3}{4}$ feet, $4\frac{5}{6}$ feet, $4\frac{2}{3}$ feet, and $4\frac{5}{12}$ feet. Use a number line to estimate fractions.

Estimate $5\frac{3}{4}$ to the nearest whole number.

Place the fractional part of the mixed number on the number line.

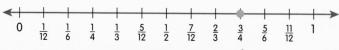

Compare the fractional part to $\frac{1}{2}$.

$$\frac{3}{4} > \frac{1}{2}$$

When the fractional part of the number is $\frac{1}{2}$ or greater, add a one to the whole number.

$5\frac{3}{4}$ rounds to $5 + 1$, or 6.

Estimate $4\frac{5}{12}$ to the nearest whole number.

Compare the fractional part to $\frac{1}{2}$.

$$\frac{5}{12} < \frac{1}{2}$$

When the fractional part of the number is less than $\frac{1}{2}$, the whole number remains the same.

$4\frac{5}{12}$ rounds to 4.

estimation — An opinion or judgment; a best guess.

Find the estimated average of your friends' heights.

Round each height to the nearest whole number.

Height	Compare the fractional part to $\frac{1}{2}$.	Round to the nearest whole number.
$5\frac{3}{4}$	$\frac{3}{4} > \frac{1}{2}$	$5 + 1 = 6$
$4\frac{3}{4}$	$\frac{3}{4} > \frac{1}{2}$	$4 + 1 = 5$
$4\frac{5}{6}$	$\frac{5}{6} > \frac{1}{2}$	$4 + 1 = 5$
$4\frac{2}{3}$	$\frac{2}{3} > \frac{1}{2}$	$4 + 1 = 5$
$4\frac{5}{12}$	$\frac{15}{2} < \frac{1}{2}$	4

The average is the sum of items divided by the number of items.

$$\text{Average} = \frac{6 + 5 + 5 + 5 + 4}{5} = \frac{25}{5}$$

$$\text{Average} = 5 \text{ feet}$$

The estimated average height for your five friends is 5 feet.

Conduct a survey. Find the average estimated height of five of your friends. What is the average estimated height of your family or your entire class?

average — A number that represents the whole group. It is the sum of all the parts divided by the number of parts.

Percents are a part of everyday life. You see percents in newspaper ads (20% OFF ON ALL SNEAKERS) and in news reports ("25% are in favor of the change"). *Percent* means "per hundred."

Suppose one half of your class passed a math test. What percent does this represent?

Changing a Fraction to a Percent

To change a fraction to a percent, multiply the fraction by 100% and reduce to lowest terms.

Change $\frac{1}{2}$ to a percent.

Step 1: Multiply the fraction by 100%.
$$\frac{1}{2} \times \frac{100\%}{1} = \frac{100\%}{2}$$

Step 2: Reduce to lowest terms.
$$\frac{100\%}{2} = 50\% \quad (100\% \div 2 = 50\%)$$

One half is the same as 50 percent. Fifty percent of the class passed the math test.

You can change $\frac{1}{2}$ to a percent by using another method: finding an equivalent fraction with a denominator of 100.
$$\frac{1}{2} = \frac{?}{100}$$

Two times what number will give you 100? (50)
$$\frac{1}{2} = \frac{1 \times 50}{2 \times 50} = \frac{50}{100}$$

$\frac{50}{100}$ is read as 50 out of 100, or 50%.

Since 100% means "100 out of 100 equal parts," 100% represents one whole. Therefore, $\frac{100\%}{1}$ is the same as $\frac{1}{1}$, or 1.

Changing Fractions to Percents

Change $\frac{1}{3}$ to a percent.

Step 1: Multiply the fraction by 100%. Write 100% as a fraction.

$$\frac{1}{3} \times \frac{100\%}{1} = \frac{100\%}{3}$$

Step 2: Divide. How many 3s are there in 10?
(3) Multiply (3 × 3 = 9). Subtract
(10 − 9 = 1). Bring down the zero.
How many 3s are there in 10?
(3) Subtract (10 − 9 = 1).

$$\begin{array}{r} 33 \\ 3\overline{)100} \\ -9 \\ \hline 10 \\ -9 \\ \hline 1 \end{array}$$

Step 3: Place the remainder (1) over the denominator (3) and add the % symbol: $33\frac{1}{3}\%$

Change $\frac{5}{3}$ to a percent.

Step 1: Multiply the fraction by 100%. Write 100% as a fraction.

$$\frac{5}{3} \times \frac{100\%}{1} = \frac{500\%}{3}$$

Step 2: Divide.

Percents are cool.

$$\begin{array}{r} 166 \\ 3\overline{)500} \\ -3 \\ \hline 20 \\ -18 \\ \hline 20 \\ -18 \\ \hline 2 \end{array}$$

Step 3: Place the remainder (2) over the denominator (3) and add the % symbol: $\frac{500}{3} = 166\frac{2}{3}\%$

---

mixed percent — A mixed number, such as $33\frac{1}{3}$, written with a percent (%) symbol. $33\frac{1}{3}\%$ is a mixed percent.

A ratio is used to compare two quantities, such as the number of circles and the number of squares.

○ ○ ○ ▢ ▢ ▢ ▢

You can write the ratio of circles to squares in three different ways:

fraction	words	colon
$\frac{3}{4}$	3 to 4	3 : 4

The fraction bar and the colon are read as "to." The numbers 3 and 4 are called the terms of the ratio. The first term is 3 and the second term is 4.

The order in which the numbers in a ratio are written is important. In this problem we are comparing circles to squares. The number of circles must be written as the first term and the number of squares as the second term.

Let's reverse the order. Compare the number of squares to the number of circles.

fraction	words	colon
$\frac{4}{3}$	4 to 3	4 : 3

The ratios are not the same when you reverse the order.

Writing Equal Ratios

Write three equal ratios for $\frac{5}{6}$.

Finding equal ratios is the same thing as finding equivalent fractions. To find equal ratios, multiply the numerator and the denominator by the same number.

1st equal ratio	2nd equal ratio	3rd equal ratio
$\frac{5 \times 2}{6 \times 2} = \frac{10}{12}$	$\frac{5 \times 3}{6 \times 3} = \frac{15}{18}$	$\frac{5 \times 4}{6 \times 4} = \frac{20}{24}$

With each ratio, think of the fraction that goes with it. Suppose the ratio of boys to girls in a store is 30 to 40, or 30 : 40. As a fraction, that's $\frac{30}{40}$, or $\frac{3}{4}$.

Reducing Ratios

To reduce a ratio to its lowest terms, divide both terms by the greatest common factor.

Reduce 30 : 45

Step 1: Find the greatest common factor (GCF) of both terms.
factors of 30:   1, 2, 3, 5, 6, 10, **15**, 30
factors of 45:   1, 3, 5, 9, **15**, 45

Step 2: Divide both terms by their GCF (15).

$$30 \div 15 : 45 \div 15$$
$$2 : 3$$
$$30 : 45 \text{ reduces to } 2 : 3.$$

Finding the Ratio of Units of Measure

Suppose you are 5 feet tall and your arm measures 20 inches. What is the ratio of your height to your arm length? The two quantities have to be expressed in the same units.

Find the ratio of 5 feet to 20 inches.

Step 1: Change 5 feet to inches. Since there are 12 inches in one foot, multiply 5 by 12. 5×12 inches = 60 inches

Step 2: Write the ratio of your height to your arm length.
60 inches to 20 inches

Step 3: Reduce both terms by the greatest common factor.
$$(60 \div 20) \text{ to } (20 \div 20)$$
$$3 \text{ to } 1$$

The ratio of your height to your arm length is 3 to 1.

Remember that ratios are equivalent when their fractions are equal.
30 : 40 and 75 : 100 are equivalent ratios since
$30 : 40 = \frac{30}{40} = \frac{3}{4}$ and $75 : 100 = \frac{75}{100} = \frac{3}{4}$.

Decimals are used in science, industry, and our monetary system to represent fractional parts. To understand decimals, let's first review place value.

A **decimal number** is a number with a decimal point.

Examples: 1.6   0.48   300.2

A **decimal fraction** is a number to the right of a decimal point. A decimal fraction is less than one.

Examples: 0.6   0.48   0.2

A **mixed decimal fraction** contains a whole number and a decimal fraction.

Examples: 6.9   30.6   100.43

Before you read and write decimal numbers, let's place one in a place value chart.

Decimal number: 91,346.52078

PLACE VALUE

Digit	In Words	Standard Form
9	ten thousands	90,000
1	thousands	1,000
3	hundreds	300
4	tens	40
6	ones	6
.	decimal point	.
5	tenths	0.5
2	hundredths	0.02
0	thousandths	0.000
7	ten thousandths	0.0007
8	hundred thousandths	0.00008

Decimals in science: 0.325g of aspirin.
Decimals in money: $0.75 , $1.25 , $10.59.

Reading Decimals

Read the decimal fraction 0.908

Read the number to the right of the decimal point as a whole number ("nine hundred eight"). Read the place value of the last digit on the right ("thousandths"). The decimal fraction is read, "Nine hundred eight thousandths."

Read the mixed decimal number 13.67

Read the number to the left of the decimal point ("thirteen"). Read the decimal point ("and"). Read the number to the right of the decimal point ("sixty-seven hundredths"). So, 13.67 is read, "Thirteen and sixty-seven hundredths."

Writing Decimals

Write eighty-nine thousandths as a decimal fraction.
Write the whole number.

89

To move the 9 to the thousandths place, add one zero before the eight and mark the decimal point to the left of that zero. Write a zero before the decimal point to serve as a placeholder.

0.089

Write fourteen and six hundredths.
Write the digits before the word *and* as a whole number.

14

Place a decimal point for the word *and*, then write the decimal fraction.   14.06

Don't forget the placeholders!
| 0.6 = six tenths | 0.06 = six hundredths |

0.006 = six thousandths

Have you ever compared batting averages or prices of different items? If you have, then you were comparing decimals.

Comparing Decimals

Compare 15.63 and 15.6

Step 1: Line up the decimal points.

$$15.6$$

$$15.63$$

Step 2: Add zeros to give each number the same number of digits. The zero is used as a placeholder and is written to the right of the last digit after the decimal point.

$$15.6\mathbf{0}$$

$$15.63$$

Step 3: Read the number from left to right until you find different digits in the same place value position. In this example, all the digits are the same except for those in the hundredths place.

Step 4: Compare the numerals using the inequality symbols.

$$15.63 > 15.60$$

Fifteen and sixty-three hundredths is greater than fifteen and sixty hundredths.

Adding zeros to the right end of a decimal number will not change its value.

Ordering Decimals

To order decimals, compare two numerals at a time and list them from least to greatest.

Order 3.102, 6.92, 3.12, and 6.82 from least to greatest.

Step 1: Line up the decimal points and add zeros where necessary to give the numbers the same number of digits.

| 3.102 |
| 3.12**0** |
| 6.92**0** |
| 6.82**0** |

Step 2: Compare the numbers two at a time. The numbers have the same digits in the ones and tenths places. They have different digits in the hundredths place.

3.1**0**2
3.1**2**0

$0 < 2$

Step 3: Compare two more numbers. They have the same digits in the ones place. They have different digits in the tenths place.

6.**9**2
6.**8**2

$8 < 9$

Step 4: Order the numbers from least to greatest.

3.102, 3.12, 6.82, 6.92

Is the numeral with the most digits the greatest number? The numeral with the most digits is 3.102. The greatest number is 6.92. The number with the most digits is not the largest number.

Place value determines which number is greatest.

When ordering decimal numbers, compare the digits in the place value positions.

16 Rounding Decimals

Calculating sums can be quick and easy when you use round numbers. You may use rounding when you go to your favorite store. It will help you find out whether you have enough money to buy all the items you would like. Rounding numbers with decimals is like rounding whole numbers.

Round 4132.78 to the nearest tenth.

Step 1: Underline the number in the tenths place.

4132.78

Step 2: Look at the number to the right of the underlined number. If that number is 5 or greater, add 1 to the underlined number. Drop all digits to the right of the underlined number.

$$\begin{array}{r} 4132.78 \\ + \underline{1} \\ \hline 4132.8 \end{array}$$

4132.78 rounded to the nearest tenth is 4132.8.

If the number to the right had been less than 5, the underlined number would stay the same and you would have dropped all numbers to the right of the underlined number.

To round decimals you must be familiar with place value.
See page 32.

Rounding Money

Suppose you wanted to buy the following items:

Book, $19.34   **Video, $16.98**   **T-shirt, $18.50**

Before you go to the cashier, you check to see whether you have enough money. You have $57.00. Will that be enough?

Round each item to the nearest dollar (ones place).

Step 1: Underline the digit in the ones place.

$1\underline{9}.34$ $1\underline{6}.98$ $1\underline{8}.50$

Step 2: If the digit to the right of the underlined digit is less than 5, keep the underlined digit. If the digit to the right of the underlined digit is 5 or greater, add one to the underlined digit. Drop all digits to the right of the underlined digit.

19.34 rounds to 19

16.98 rounds to 17
$$\begin{array}{r} \$1\underline{6}.98 \\ +\ 1 \\ \hline \$17 \end{array}$$

18.50 rounds to 19
$$\begin{array}{r} \$1\underline{8}.50 \\ +\ 1 \\ \hline \$19 \end{array}$$

Step 3: Add the rounded numbers. $19 + 17 + 19 = 55$
You would spend approximately $55.

Is this answer close to the exact cost? Let's find the actual sum of the three items.

Line up the decimal points and place the decimal in the sum.

$$\begin{array}{r} \$19.34 \\ \$16.98 \\ +\ \$18.50 \\ \hline \$54.82 \end{array} \leftarrow \textbf{exact}$$

Rounding to the nearest dollar ($55) is close to the exact sum ($54.82).

round number — A number written in terms of the nearest whole number, or nearest ten, hundred, tenth, etc. The number 600 is the round number of 568, and 6 is the round number of $5\frac{2}{3}$.

Suppose you had a batting average of 0.125. What fraction of the time do you get a hit when you come up to bat?

Write 0.125 as a fraction.

Step 1: Write the digits to the right of the decimal point as a whole number. Place it in the numerator.

$$\underline{125}$$

Step 2: Determine the place value of the digit farthest to the right of the decimal point (5). If it is in the tenths place, write 10 in the denominator. If it is in the hundredths place, write 100 in the denominator, and so on. The 5 is in the thousandths place. Place 1,000 in the denominator.

$$\frac{125}{1,000}$$

Step 3: Reduce the numerator and denominator by the greatest common factor.

$$\frac{125 \div 125}{1000 \div 125} = \frac{1}{8}$$

When you come up to bat, you get a hit one eighth of the time. One out of every eight at-bats is a hit. If you did not reduce the fraction to lowest terms, then you would get one hundred twenty-five hits out of every one thousand at-bats.

You can review greatest common factors (GCF) on page 9.

Renaming a Mixed Decimal as a Mixed Number

Write 17.6 as a mixed number.

Step 1: Write the whole number.   17

Step 2: Read the decimal fraction (six tenths). $17\frac{6}{10}$
Place the 6 in the numerator and
10 in the denominator.

Step 3: Reduce the fraction to lowest $17\frac{(6 \div 2)}{(10 \div 2)} = 17\frac{3}{5}$
terms by dividing the numerator
and denominator by their greatest
common factor.

17.6 is the same as $17\frac{3}{5}$

Write 123.005 as a mixed number.

Step 1: Write the whole number.   123

Step 2: Read the decimal fraction (five thousandths). $123\frac{5}{1,000}$
Place the 5 in the numerator and 1,000 in the
denominator.

Step 3: Reduce the fraction to lowest $123\frac{5 \div 5}{1000 \div 5}$
terms by dividing the numerator
and denominator by their greatest $123\frac{1}{200}$
common factor.

Find out the batting average of your favorite baseball player. What fraction of the time does he get a hit when he gets up to bat?

mixed number — A whole number and a fraction.
decimal fraction — A fraction with a denominator of 10, 100, 1,000, or 10,000. . . .

Some of the produce available at the supermarket are tomatoes, string beans, lettuce, zucchini, and collard greens. Which vegetable do you think sells for the most money per pound?

vegetable	price per pound
tomatoes	1.59
string beans	0.79
lettuce	0.89
zucchini	0.66
collards	0.99

From the list above, tomatoes cost the most money. The numerals in the list are decimal fractions. Adding decimal fractions is like adding whole numbers. The only difference is lining up the decimal points.

Add the cost per pound for lettuce and zucchini.

Step 1: Write the numbers vertically so that the decimal points line up.

$$\begin{array}{r} 0.89 \\ +\ 0.66 \\ \hline \end{array}$$

Step 2: Add the numbers in the same way you add whole numbers and place the decimal point in the sum.

$$\begin{array}{r} 0.89 \\ +\ 0.66 \\ \hline 1.55 \end{array}$$

The cost for a pound of lettuce and a pound of zucchini is $1.55.

Whole numbers and decimal fractions are both added in the order of their place value.

Adding Whole Numbers and Mixed Decimals

To add a whole number and a mixed decimal, follow the same procedure as adding decimal fractions. It is very important to remember to place a decimal point after the whole number and add as many zeros as necessary.

Add 2 + 1.2 + 12.46 + 103.01

Step 1: Align the decimals vertically. Add zeros so that each number has the same number of places to the right of the decimal.

$$\begin{array}{r} 2.00 \\ 1.20 \\ 12.46 \\ +\ 103.01 \end{array}$$

Step 2: Starting at the right, add the numbers the same way you would add whole numbers. Place a decimal point in the sum.

$$\begin{array}{r} 2.00 \\ 1.20 \\ 12.46 \\ +\ 103.01 \\ \hline 118.67 \end{array}$$

Adding Decimal Fractions and Whole Numbers

Add 0.3 + 5 + 0.1325 + 13

Step 1: Align the decimals vertically. Add zeros so that each number has the same number of places to the right of the decimal.

$$\begin{array}{r} 0.3000 \\ 5.0000 \\ 0.1325 \\ +\ 13.0000 \end{array}$$

Step 2: Starting at the right, add the numbers the same way you would add whole numbers. Place a decimal point in the sum.

$$\begin{array}{r} 0.3000 \\ 5.0000 \\ 0.1325 \\ +\ 13.0000 \\ \hline 18.4325 \end{array}$$

Always line up decimal points when adding decimals. Remember to include the decimal point in your answer.

Adding Decimals with Regrouping

Stopwatches are used to time races. They are accurate to one tenth of a second. Suppose your track team is competing against your best friend's team in the 60-yard dash. Your job is to find out which team is faster. You decide to make a chart of each runner's time.

| Team A | 9.6 | 17.9 | 16 | 17.2 |
| Team B | 9.7 | 15.3 | 20 | 15.8 |

Adding decimals with regrouping is similar to adding whole numbers with regrouping. The only difference is lining up the decimal points.

Column Addition

Use column addition to determine the faster team.

Step 1: Add Team A's times. Line up the decimal points. Write a decimal point after any whole numbers. Add a zero to the right of that decimal point.

$$\begin{array}{r} 9.6 \\ 17.9 \\ 16.0 \\ + 17.2 \\ \hline \end{array}$$

Step 2: Add the tenths column. Place the 7 in the tenths column and regroup the 1 to the ones column.

$$\begin{array}{r} 1 \\ 9.6 \\ 17.9 \\ 16.0 \\ + 17.2 \\ \hline 7 \end{array}$$

Step 3: Place the decimal point in the sum. Add the ones column. Place the zero in the ones column and regroup the 3 to the tens column.

$$\begin{array}{r} 31 \\ 9.6 \\ 17.9 \\ 16.0 \\ + 17.2 \\ \hline 0.7 \end{array}$$

The only difference between adding decimals and adding whole numbers is the decimal point.

Step 4: Add the tens column.

$$\begin{array}{r} ^{31} \\ 9.6 \\ 17.9 \\ 16.0 \\ +\ 17.2 \\ \hline 60.7 \end{array}$$

The total time for Team A is 60.7 seconds.

Step 5: Add Team B's times. Line up the decimal points. Place a decimal point after any whole numbers and add a zero. Add tenths. Regroup (18 tenths = 1 one 8 tenths). Place the 8 in the tenths column and regroup the one to the ones column.

$$\begin{array}{r} ^{1} \\ 9.7 \\ 15.3 \\ 20.0 \\ +\ 15.8 \\ \hline 8 \end{array}$$

Step 6: Place the decimal in the sum. Add ones. Regroup (20 ones = 2 tens 0 ones). Place the zero in the ones column and regroup the two to the tens column.

$$\begin{array}{r} ^{21} \\ 9.7 \\ 15.3 \\ 20.0 \\ +\ 15.2 \\ \hline 0.8 \end{array}$$

Step 7: Add tens.

$$\begin{array}{r} ^{21} \\ 9.7 \\ 15.3 \\ 20.0 \\ +\ 15.2 \\ \hline 60.8 \end{array}$$

The total time for Team B is 60.8 seconds.

Step 8: Compare times.

$$60.7 \text{ seconds} < 60.8 \text{ seconds}$$

The faster team is Team A.

Practice adding decimals the next time you visit the mall. You can add prices of your favorite items.

Does your bicycle record the distance you ride? Some bikes record cycling distances to the nearest tenth of a kilometer. Cyclists keep a record of the kilometers they cycle. They usually increase their distance each week until they reach their goal. Cyclists use subtraction of decimal numbers to compare their weekly distance.

Subtracting Decimal Fractions

A decimal fraction is a number less than one, such as 0.8, 0.12, and 0.468. Let's subtract two decimal fractions.

Subtract 0.8 − 0.3

Step 1: Line up the decimal points.

$$\begin{array}{r} 0.8 \\ -\,0.3 \\ \hline \end{array}$$

Step 2: Subtract as you would whole numbers. Place the decimal point in the difference.

$$\begin{array}{r} 0.8 \\ -\,0.3 \\ \hline 0.5 \end{array}$$

Subtracting a Mixed Decimal and a Decimal Fraction

Subtract 5.6 − 0.4

Step 1: Line up the decimal points. Subtract tenths. Place the decimal point in the answer.

$$\begin{array}{r} 5.6 \\ -\,0.4 \\ \hline .2 \end{array}$$

Step 2: Subtract ones.

$$\begin{array}{r} 5.6 \\ -\,0.4 \\ \hline 5.2 \end{array}$$

decimal fraction — A fraction with a denominator of 10, 100, 1,000, 10,000 . . . such as $\frac{3}{10}$ or $\frac{20}{100}$. They can easily be written as decimals. $\frac{3}{10} = 0.3$; $\frac{20}{100} = 0.20$.

Subtracting a Mixed Decimal and a Whole Number

To write a whole number as a decimal, place a decimal point to the right of the whole number and add one or more zeros.

Subtract 72.98 − 11

Step 1: Place a decimal point to the right of the whole number. Line up the decimal points. Add two zeros to the right of the decimal point

$$\begin{array}{r} 72.98 \\ -\,11.00 \\ \hline \end{array}$$

Step 2: Subtract hundredths.

$$\begin{array}{r} 72.98 \\ -\,11.00 \\ \hline 8 \end{array}$$

Step 3: Subtract tenths. Place the decimal point in the difference.

$$\begin{array}{r} 72.98 \\ -\,11.00 \\ \hline .98 \end{array}$$

Step 4: Subtract ones.

$$\begin{array}{r} 72.98 \\ -\,11.00 \\ \hline 1.98 \end{array}$$

Step 5: Subtract tens.

$$\begin{array}{r} 72.98 \\ -\,11.00 \\ \hline 61.98 \end{array}$$

Using a metric tape, measure your arm from shoulder to fingertip. Then measure each family member's arm. Who has the shortest arm? Who has the longest? Find the difference between the longest and shortest arm.

Just a reminder...

Remember, a mixed decimal contains a whole number with a decimal, such as 72.98.

21 Subtracting Decimals with Regrouping

An odometer is an instrument that measures distance traveled. Ask a family member to record the car odometer reading before he or she leaves the house in the morning. When he or she comes home in the evening, check the new odometer reading.

Suppose the morning odometer reading is 5678.9 and the evening odometer reading is 5743.1. How far did the person drive? To find the distance traveled, subtract the morning reading from the evening reading.

Subtracting Mixed Decimal Numbers

A mixed decimal number contains a whole number and a decimal fraction. Examples of mixed decimal numbers are the morning and evening odometer readings.

Let's find the distance traveled.

Subtract 5743.1 − 5678.9

Step 1: Line up the decimal points.

$$\begin{array}{r} 5743.1 \\ -\ 5678.9 \end{array}$$

Step 2: Subtract tenths. Regroup ones
(1 one = 10 tenths).
10 tenths + 1 tenth = 11 tenths
11 − 9 = 2

$$\begin{array}{r} {}^{2}\ {}^{11} \\ 574\cancel{3}.\cancel{1} \\ -\ 5678.9 \\ \hline 2 \end{array}$$

The only difference between subtracting decimals and subtracting whole numbers is the decimal point. Just remember to place the decimal point in your final answer.

Step 3: Place the decimal in the difference.
Subtract ones. Regroup tens
(1 ten = 10 ones).
10 ones + 2 ones = 12 ones 12 − 8 = 4

$$\begin{array}{r} {\scriptstyle 31211} \\ 57\mathbf{43}.\mathbf{\cancel{1}} \\ -\ 5678.9 \\ \hline \mathbf{4}.2 \end{array}$$

Step 4: Subtract tens. Regroup hundreds
(1 hundred = 10 tens)
10 tens + 3 tens = 13 tens
13 − 7 = 6

$$\begin{array}{r} {\scriptstyle 6131211} \\ 5\mathbf{743}.\mathbf{\cancel{1}} \\ -\ 5678.9 \\ \hline \mathbf{6}4.2 \end{array}$$

Step 5: Subtract hundreds (6 − 6 = 0).
Subtract thousands (5 − 5 = 0).
You do not need a zero in the
hundreds or thousands place.

$$\begin{array}{r} {\scriptstyle 6131211} \\ \mathbf{57}43.\mathbf{\cancel{1}} \\ -\ \mathbf{56}78.9 \\ \hline 64.2 \end{array}$$

Your family member drove 64.2 miles.

You can check your answer by adding it to the morning odometer reading. If the sum is equal to the evening odometer reading, then your answer is correct.

Don't forget to check your answers.

$$\begin{array}{r} 5678.9 \\ +\quad 64.2 \\ \hline 5743.1 \end{array}$$

morning odometer reading
miles driven
evening odometer reading

A great way to check your subtraction answer is to add your answer to the number you subtracted:

$$\text{If } A - B = C \text{ then } C + B = A$$

Suppose you walk seven tenths of a mile to school each day. On the way home you take the bus. How many miles do you walk to school each week?

Multiplying a Whole Number by a Decimal

When you multiply decimal numbers, you do not have to line up the decimal points.

Multiply 5 × 0.7

Step 1: Write the factors in a vertical format. Count the number of decimal places in each factor.

$$\begin{array}{r} 5 \\ \times\ 0.7 \end{array}$$

0 decimal places
1 decimal place

Step 2: Multiply as you would whole numbers. Find the sum of the number of decimal places in the factors.

$$\begin{array}{r} 5 \\ \times\ 0.7 \\ \hline 35 \end{array}$$

0 decimal places
1 decimal place
1 decimal place

Step 3: Counting from right to left, place the decimal point in the product one place to the left, since 1 was the sum of decimal places in the factors.

$$\begin{array}{r} 5 \\ \times\ 0.7 \\ \hline 3.5 \end{array}$$

0 decimal places
1 decimal place
1 decimal place

You walk 3.5 miles to school each week.

factors — The numbers being multiplied.
product — The answer in a multiplication problem.

Multiplying a Mixed Decimal by a Decimal Fraction

Sometimes your answer (the product) may not contain as many digits as the sum of the decimal places in the factor. In that case, place as many zeros to the left of the digits in the product as needed to place the decimal point.

Multiply 6.3 × 0.002

Step 1: Write the factors in a vertical format. Count the number of decimal places in each factor.

$$\begin{array}{r} 6.3 \\ \times\ 0.002 \end{array}$$ **1 decimal place**
3 decimal places

Step 2: Multiply as you would whole numbers. Add the the number of decimal places in the factors.

$$\begin{array}{r} 6.3 \\ \times\ 0.002 \\ \hline 126 \end{array}$$ **1 decimal places**
3 decimal places
4 decimal places

Step 3: Counting from right to left, place the decimal point in the product.

$$\begin{array}{r} 6.3 \\ \times\ 0.002 \\ \hline 0.0126 \end{array}$$ **decimal place**
3 decimal places
4 decimal places

Since you need 4 decimal places and there are only 3 digits in the product, add a zero to the left of the digits to place the decimal point. The zero before the decimal point serves as a placeholder to let the reader know that there are no ones.

How far do you walk or ride from home to school each week?

When placing the decimal point in your answer, always start at the end of the digit. Count to the left the correct number of decimal places: .0 1 2 6
4 3 2 1

How many ounces of water do you drink each day? Suppose you drank 331.1 ounces of water over one week. On average, how many ounces of water do you drink each day?

Dividing a Mixed Decimal by a Whole Number

Divide 331.1 ounces by 7 days.

Step 1: Place the decimal point in the quotient directly above the decimal point in the dividend.

$$7\overline{)331.1} \quad \leftarrow \text{quotient} \atop \leftarrow \text{dividend}$$

Step 2: Divide. How many 7s are there in 33? (4) Multiply ($4 \times 7 = 28$). Subtract ($33 - 28 = 5$).

$$\begin{array}{r} 4. \\ 7\overline{)331.1} \\ -28 \\ \hline 5 \end{array}$$

Step 3: Bring down the next digit in the dividend (1). Divide. How many 7s are there in 51? (7) Multiply ($7 \times 7 = 49$). Subtract ($51 - 49 = 2$). Bring down the next digit (1). Divide, multiply, and subtract again.

$$\begin{array}{r} 47.3 \\ 7\overline{)331.1} \\ -28 \\ \hline 51 \\ -49 \\ \hline 21 \\ -21 \\ \hline 0 \end{array}$$

You drank an average of 47.3 ounces of water each day.

When you move the decimal point one place to the right, that's the same as multiplying the number by 10.

quotient — The answer in a division problem.

Dividing Two Whole Numbers

Divide 4 by 8

Step 1: Since the answer is less than one, place a decimal point after the whole number in the dividend and add a zero to the right of the decimal point. Place the decimal point in the quotient.

$$8\overline{)4.0} \quad \leftarrow \text{quotient} \\ \leftarrow \text{dividend}$$

Step 2: Divide. How many 8s are there in 4? (Zero) How many 8s are there in 40? (5) Multiply $(5 \times 8 = 40)$. Subtract $(40 - 40 = 0)$.

$$\begin{array}{r} 0.5 \\ 8\overline{)4.0} \\ -\,4.0 \\ \hline 0 \end{array}$$

Dividing Two Decimal Fractions

Divide 0.028 by 0.7

Step 1: Move the decimal point one place to the right in the divisor to make it a whole number. Then move the decimal point in the dividend one place to the right. Place the decimal point in the quotient.

$$\text{divisor} \rightarrow 0.7\overline{)0.028} \leftarrow \text{dividend}$$

$$7\overline{)00.28} \quad \leftarrow \text{quotient}$$

Step 2: Divide, multiply, and subtract.

$$\begin{array}{r} 0.04 \\ 7\overline{)0.28} \\ -\,28 \\ \hline 0 \end{array}$$

As long as you multiply both the divisor and the dividend by the same number, the value of the quotient will not change. It is the same as multiplying by 1.

Multiplying and Dividing Decimals by Powers of Ten

In mathematics there are times when you have to multiply or divide a decimal by 10, 100, 1000, 10,000, etc. These numbers are called powers of ten. They always include a one followed by one or more zeros. You can use a shortcut when you multiply or divide by powers of ten. This shortcut only works when one of the factors is a power of ten.

Multiplying a Decimal by a Power of Ten

To multiply a decimal by a power of ten, move the decimal point in the decimal number **to the right** as many places as there are zeros in the power of ten. Look at the following examples:

Multiply by a power of ten.	Move the decimal to the right.	Example
10	1 place	$2.78 \times 10 = 27.8$
100	2 places	$2.78 \times 100 = 278$
1,000	3 places	$2.78 \times 1,000 = 2,780$
10,000	4 places	$2.78 \times 10,000 = 27,800$
100,000	5 places	$2.78 \times 100,000 = 278,000$
1,000,000	6 places	$2.78 \times 1,000,000 = 2,780,000$

Can you see any patterns in the above examples? The decimal point changes position when you multiply by a power of ten. The larger the power of ten, the greater the product or answer. This shortcut does not require you to multiply the factors. It allows you to move the decimal point to the right in the decimal number as many places as there are zeros in the power of ten.

It is much easier to move the decimal point when multiplying by a power of 10 rather than actually multiplying all those numbers.

Dividing Decimal Numbers by Powers of Ten

To divide a decimal by a power of ten (10, 100, 1,000, . . .), move the decimal point in the decimal number **to the left** as many places as there are zeros in the power of ten. Look at the following examples:

Divide by a power of ten.	Move the decimal to the left.	Example
10	1 place	$2.78 \div 10 = 0.278$
100	2 places	$2.78 \div 100 = 0.0278$
1,000	3 places	$2.78 \div 1,000 = 0.00278$
10,000	4 places	$2.78 \div 10,000 = 0.000278$
100,000	5 places	$2.78 \div 100,000 = 0.0000278$
1,000,000	6 places	$2.78 \div 1,000,000 = 0.00000278$

Do you see any patterns? The decimal point changes position when you divide by powers of ten. The larger the power of ten, the smaller the quotient. This shortcut does not require you to divide the numbers. It allows you to move the decimal point to the left in the decimal number as many places as there are zeros in the power of ten.

Multiplying and Dividing by Powers of Ten

Multiply and divide a decimal number by a power of ten.

Multiply by 10: $32.5 \times 10 = 325$

Divide by 10: $32.5 \div 10 = 3.25$

Multiplying moves the decimal point to the right. Dividing moves the decimal point to the left.

An estimate is an approximation of the exact answer. You can estimate sums, differences, products, and quotients to determine if the answer is reasonable.

Methods Used to Estimate Sums

A. By rounding to the greatest place of the larger number:

$$
\begin{array}{r}
2.485 \\
+\ 0.562 \\
\end{array}
\qquad
\begin{array}{r}
2 \\
+\ 1 \\
\hline
3 \\
\end{array}
\;\longleftarrow \textbf{estimated sum}
$$

B. By rounding to the greatest place of the smaller number:

$$
\begin{array}{r}
2.485 \\
+\ 0.562 \\
\end{array}
\qquad
\begin{array}{r}
2.5 \\
+\ 0.6 \\
\hline
3.1 \\
\end{array}
\;\longleftarrow \textbf{estimated sum}
$$

C. By rounding to a specified decimal place, such as hundredths.

$$
\begin{array}{r}
2.485 \\
+\ 0.562 \\
\end{array}
\qquad
\begin{array}{r}
2.49 \\
+\ 0.56 \\
\hline
3.05 \\
\end{array}
\;\longleftarrow \textbf{estimated sum}
$$

In the example, the greatest place value of the larger number is the ones place. The greatest place value of the smaller number is tenths. When rounding to a specified place value you can choose any place value position.

Estimating Differences

Let's use the same example, but now subtract.

$$
2.485 - 0.562 \qquad \text{A.}\ \begin{array}{r} 2 \\ -\ 1 \\ \hline 1 \end{array} \qquad \text{B.}\ \begin{array}{r} 2.5 \\ -\ 0.6 \\ \hline 1.9 \end{array} \qquad \text{C.}\ \begin{array}{r} 2.49 \\ -\ 0.56 \\ \hline 1.93 \end{array}
$$

Estimating to the nearest hundredth gives the closest answer to the exact sum and difference.

$$
\begin{array}{r}
2.485 \\
+\ 0.562 \\
\hline
3.047 \\
\end{array}
\;\longleftarrow \textbf{exact sum}
\qquad\qquad
\begin{array}{r}
2.485 \\
-\ 0.562 \\
\hline
1.923 \\
\end{array}
\;\longleftarrow \textbf{exact difference}
$$

The methods for estimating sums and differences also work for adding and subtracting more than two numbers.

Estimating Products and Quotients

Estimate the product of 6.4 × 0.82

Estimating products and quotients is also done by several methods:

A. By rounding to the greatest place of the larger number:

$$\begin{array}{r} 6.40 \\ \times\ 0.82 \\ \hline \end{array} \qquad \begin{array}{r} 6 \\ \times\ 1 \\ \hline 6 \end{array} \longleftarrow \textbf{estimated product}$$

B. By rounding to the greatest place of the smaller number:

$$\begin{array}{r} 6.40 \\ \times\ 0.82 \\ \hline \end{array} \qquad \begin{array}{r} 6.4 \\ \times\ 0.8 \\ \hline 5.12 \end{array} \longleftarrow \textbf{estimated product}$$

C. By rounding each number to its greatest place value.

$$\begin{array}{r} 6.40 \\ \times\ 0.82 \\ \hline \end{array} \qquad \begin{array}{r} 6 \\ \times\ 0.8 \\ \hline 4.8 \end{array} \longleftarrow \textbf{estimated product}$$

The exact product of 6.4 × 0.82 is 5.248. Estimating to the greatest place of the smaller number (5.12) is closest to the exact answer.

Now find the estimated quotient for the same example.

A. 6.4 ÷ 0.82   6 ÷ 1 = 6

B. 6.4 ÷ 0.82   6.4 ÷ 0.8 = 8

C. 6.4 ÷ 0.82   6 ÷ 0.8 = 7.5

The exact quotient of 6.42 ÷ 0.8 is 8.025.
Estimating to the greatest place of the smaller number is closest to the exact answer.

---

quotient — The answer in a division problem.

$$703 \longleftarrow \textbf{quotient}$$
$$\textbf{divisor} \longrightarrow 6\overline{)4218} \longleftarrow \textbf{dividend}$$

Fractions $\left(\frac{3}{4}, \frac{9}{8}\right)$ and mixed numbers $\left(1\frac{2}{3}, 2\frac{1}{4}\right)$ can be written as repeating or terminating decimals by changing the fraction to a decimal.

Terminating Decimals

Change $\frac{1}{4}$ to a decimal.

Step 1: Divide the denominator into the numerator. Place a decimal point to the right of the whole number in the dividend and add zeros.

$$4\overline{)1.00}$$

Step 2: Divide ($10 \div 4 = 2$). Multiply ($2 \times 4 = 8$). Subtract ($10 - 8 = 2$). Bring down the next digit (0). Divide ($20 \div 4 = 5$). Multiply ($5 \times 4 = 20$). Subtract ($20 - 20 = 0$).

$$
\begin{array}{r}
0.25 \\
4\overline{)1.00} \\
-8 \\
\hline
20 \\
-20 \\
\hline
0
\end{array}
$$

If the remainder is zero, the quotient (answer) is called a terminating decimal. When the same remainder keeps appearing, the quotient is called a repeating decimal.

When you change $\frac{1}{4}$ to a decimal the exact quotient is 0.25. The decimal, 0.25, is called a terminating decimal because it has an exact answer. If you were changing a mixed number, such as $1\frac{1}{4}$, to a fraction, only the fraction part of the mixed number would be changed to a decimal. You can write $1\frac{1}{4}$ as 1.25. The whole number is written first, then the decimal equivalent is determined for the fractional part.

When a denominator divides evenly into its numerator, the quotient is called a **terminating decimal**.

Repeating Decimals

Change $\frac{2}{11}$ to a decimal.

Step 1: Divide the denominator into the numerator. Place a decimal point to the right of the whole number in the dividend and add zeros.

$$11\overline{)2.00}$$

Step 2: Divide (20 ÷ 11 = 1). Multiply (1 × 11 = 11). Subtract (20 − 11 = 9). Bring down the next digit (0). Divide (90 ÷ 11 = 8). Multiply (8 × 11 = 88). Subtract (90 − 88 = 2). Add two more zeros. Bring down a zero. Divide (20 ÷ 11 = 2). Multiply (8 × 11 = 88). Subtract (90 − 88 = 2).

$$
\begin{array}{r}
0.1818 \\
11\overline{)2.0000} \\
-\ 11 \\
\hline
90 \\
-\ 88 \\
\hline
20 \\
-\ 11 \\
\hline
90 \\
-\ 88 \\
\hline
2
\end{array}
$$

Step 3: Write the answer as a repeating decimal. $0.\overline{18}$

Place a bar above the digits that repeat. Notice, two remainders keep appearing (2 and 9). If you had the same fractional part in a mixed number, such as $3\frac{2}{11}$, you would write it as $3.\overline{18}$. Write the whole number, then the repeating decimal.

I get it!

When the remainder keeps appearing after you divide, the quotient is called a **repeating decimal** (see page 13).

Renaming Repeating Decimals as Fractions

How do you rename a repeating decimal as a fraction? Some repeating decimals are $0.\overline{6}$, $0.\overline{45}$ and $0.\overline{123}$. Remember, when there is a bar over the digits, it means the digits repeat. For example:

$0.\overline{45} = 0.45454545\ldots$, and $0.\overline{296} = 0.296296296296296\ldots$

Write $0.\overline{6}$ as a fraction.

Step 1: Make the repeating decimal a whole number by moving the decimal point one place to the right.

$0.\overline{6}$ becomes 6

Step 2: Use one as an exponent for 10, since we moved the decimal point one place.

exponent

$10^1 = 10$

Step 3: Subtract one from the answer in Step 2.

$10 - 1 = 9$

Step 4: Divide the number in Step 1 by the number in Step 3.

$\dfrac{6}{9}$

Step 5: Reduce the fraction to lowest terms using the greatest common factor.

$\dfrac{6 \div 3}{9 \div 3} = \dfrac{2}{3}$

Two thirds is equal to $0.\overline{6}$.

You can use a shortcut to change a repeating decimal to a fraction.

* If the repeating decimal has one digit that is repeating, place the digit over nine and reduce the fraction to lowest terms.

* If the repeating decimal has two repeating digits, place both digits over 99 and reduce the fraction to lowest terms.

* If the repeating decimal has three repeating digits, place the three digits over 999 and reduce the fraction to lowest terms.

Let's try this shortcut:

0.6 has 1 digit so place 6 over 9: $\dfrac{6}{9}$;

$\dfrac{6}{9} = \dfrac{2}{3}$. The shortcut works.

You can continue this pattern for any number of digits. Use this shortcut to change a repeating decimal to a fraction no matter how many repeating digits you have in a decimal.

Change $0.\overline{123}$ to a fraction using the shortcut.

Step 1: How many repeating digits are there in the decimal? (3) Place the digits over 999.

$$\frac{123}{999}$$

Step 2: Reduce the fraction by the greatest common factor.

$$\frac{123 \div 3}{999 \div 3} = \frac{41}{333}$$

$$0.123 = \frac{41}{333}$$

Change $0.\overline{45}$ to a fraction using the shortcut.

Step 1: How many repeating digits are there in the decimal? (2) Place the digits over 99.

$$\frac{45}{99}$$

Step 2: Reduce the fraction by the greatest common factor.

$$\frac{45 \div 9}{99 \div 9} = \frac{5}{11}$$

$$0.45 = \frac{5}{11}$$

Play "Name that Fraction"

One family member acts as a host. He or she calls out repeating decimals from a list. The players have to change the repeating decimal into a fraction. Each player challenges the other opponent. For example, one player tells his opponent that he can name that repeating decimal in 16 seconds. His opponent can either say, "Name that fraction" or she can challenge the first player by naming it in less than 16 seconds. The first player to get 3 fractions correct wins.

You can find a list of repeating decimals and their equivalent fractions in any math textbook. Some of them are:

$$\frac{1}{3} = 0.\overline{3}; \qquad \frac{5}{6} = 0.8\overline{3} \qquad \frac{6}{11} = 0.\overline{54}$$

Your body is made up of groups of cells called tissues. Some tissues that make up the human body are bone, brain, blood, heart, kidney, liver, muscle, skin, and spleen.

Can you name the tissue that makes up the largest part of the body? Can you name the tissue that makes up the smallest part of the body?

The table below shows the breakdown by weight of different types of tissue in the human body.

The Human Body

tissue	parts by weight
blood	0.07
bone	0.176
brain	0.022
heart	0.005
kidneys	0.006
liver	0.028
muscle	0.43
skin	0.26
spleen	0.003

The tissue that makes up the largest part of the body by weight is muscle. The smallest part by weight is the spleen.

When adding decimal parts of a whole unit, the decimals should add up to 1 (or 100%). For example, the values in the above table add up to 1.000, or 100%.

Changing a Decimal Number to a Percent

To change a decimal number to a percent, multiply the numeral by 100%. You can do this by moving the decimal point from its original position to two places to the right and adding a percent sign (%). Remember, when you multiply a decimal by a power of ten, you move the decimal point in the decimal number to the right as many places as there are zeros in the power of ten.

Let's change the decimal numbers in our table of tissues to percents. Multiply each decimal number by 100%, or move the decimal two places to the right.

Tissue type	Parts by weight	Multiply by 100%	Percentage of weight per tissue type
blood	0.07	0.07 × 100%	7%
bone	0.176	0.176 × 100%	17.6%
brain	0.022	0.022 × 100%	2.2%
heart	0.005	0.005 × 100%	0.5%
kidneys	0.006	0.006 × 100%	0.6%
liver	0.028	0.028 × 100%	2.8%
muscle	0.43	0.43 × 100%	43%
skin	0.26	0.26 × 100%	26%
spleen	0.003	0.003 × 100%	0.3%

Muscle makes up 43 percent by weight of the human body, and the spleen makes up 0.3 percent.

See if a family member can answer the following question. Which makes up more of the body by weight, muscle or skin?

To review multiplying decimals by powers of ten, see page 52.

Further Reading

Books

McMullen, Chris. *Practice Adding, Subtracting, Multiplying and Dividing Fractions Workbook: Improve Your Math Fluency Series.* New York: CreateSpace, 2010.

McMullen, Chris. *Radial Fractions Math Workbook (Addition and Subtraction): A Fun & Creative Visual Stategy to Practice Adding and Subtracting Fractions.* New York: CreateSpace, 2010.

Muschla, Gary and Muschla, Judith. *Practice! Practice! Practice! Fractions & Decimals: 50 Independent Practice Pages That Help Kids Master Essential Math Skills-and Meet the NCTM Standards.* New York: Teaching Resources, 2005.

Internet Addresses

Education 4 Kids. *Math Flashcards to Kids.* ©1995–2005. <http://drill.edu4kids.com/index.php?TB=2&page=12>.

Manura, David. *Math2.org.* ©1995–2005. <http://math2.org>.

The Math Forum. *Ask Dr. Math.* © 1994–2000. <http://mathforum.org/dr.math/>.

WebMath. n.d. <http://www.webmath.com/index2.html>.

Index